Evaluation of a Toyota Prius Hybrid System

U.S. Environmental Protection Agency

The BiblioGov Project is an effort to expand awareness of the public documents and records of the U.S. Government via print publications. In broadening the public understanding of government and its work, an enlightened democracy can grow and prosper. Ranging from historic Congressional Bills to the most recent Budget of the United States Government, the BiblioGov Project spans a wealth of government information. These works are now made available through an environmentally friendly, print-on-demand basis, using only what is necessary to meet the required demands of an interested public. We invite you to learn of the records of the U.S. Government, heightening the knowledge and debate that can lead from such publications.

Included are the following Collections:

Budget of The United States Government
Presidential Documents
United States Code
Education Reports from ERIC
GAO Reports
History of Bills
House Rules and Manual
Public and Private Laws

Code of Federal Regulations
Congressional Documents
Economic Indicators
Federal Register
Government Manuals
House Journal
Privacy act Issuances
Statutes at Large

United States
Environmental Protection
Agency

Air and Radiation

EPA420-R-98-006
August 1998

EPA

Evaluation of a Toyota Prius Hybrid System (THS)

EPA 420-R-98-006

Technical Report

**Evaluation of a
Toyota Prius Hybrid System (THS)**

by

**Karl H. Hellman
Maria R. Peralta
Gregory K. Piotrowski**

August 1998

NOTICE

Technical reports do not necessarily represent final EPA
decisions or positions. They are intended to present technical
analysis of issues using data which are currently available. The
purpose in the release of such reports is to facilitate the
exchange of technical information and to inform the public of
technical developments which may form the basis for a final EPA
decision, position, or regulatory action.

United States Environmental Protection Agency
Office of Air and Radiation
Office of Mobile Sources
Advanced Technology Support Division
Technology Development and Support Group
2565 Plymouth Road
Ann Arbor, MI 48105

Contents

SUMMARY

A Toyota Hybrid System (THS) vehicle was evaluated by EPA over a variety of testing modes and conditions. The THS, provided by the Toyota Motor Corporation, is a hybrid electric vehicle powered by an internal combustion engine and an alternating current synchronous motor. The hybrid system allows the engine to operate in a lower speed, higher torque, and higher efficiency mode, and enables regenerative braking recharging of the vehicle battery pack. The THS is described by Toyota as a charge sustaining hybrid, meaning that the vehicle power management system maintains the charge in the battery pack by recharging with the on-board engine. The Prius THS tested here is a Japan-market production vehicle, originally designed for the Japanese vehicle market. The THS would be classified as a subcompact-class vehicle under the United States classification, and the curb weight, with a full 50-liter fuel tank, is 2783 pounds.

Zero-60 mile-per-hour (mph) acceleration testing, as a measure of performance, was conducted. Acceleration time depended upon the state of charge of the battery pack. With a battery pack charged in a normal manner contemplated by the designers, 0-60 mph acceleration times slightly in excess of 14 seconds were measured. With a battery discharged well below the normal level of charge contemplated by the Toyota designers, 0-60 mph acceleration time increased to slightly over 19 seconds.

One important evaluation sequence consisted of two consecutive tests over the Federal Urban Dynamometer Driving Schedule (hereafter, "4-bag FTP"), followed immediately by a single test over the Highway Fuel Economy Test (HFET) cycle. This cycle is explained in Section V, Test Procedure, and is hereafter referred to as the "Number 2" test sequence.

Emission levels of hydrocarbons, carbon monoxide, and oxides of nitrogen over the 4-Bag FTP were well below current Federal light-duty vehicle emission standards. A city/highway composite fuel economy, using traditional "55/45" weighting may be described with the Number 2 test sequence above, if the measured HFET conducted immediately following the "4-bag FTP" is used for the highway fuel economy number. A 55/45 composite fuel economy calculated in this manner using the data given in this report was

iv

48.6 mpg. A variation of this test sequence is to follow the 4-bag FTP with two HFET cycles, the first, a preconditioning drive, and the second, a measured HFET (hereafter, the "Number 1" test sequence, see Section V, Test Procedure). The average city/highway (55/45) composite fuel economy calculated with data from this report over the Number 1 procedure was 49.8 mpg.

Fuel economy could be affected by the net charge/discharge of the vehicle battery pack over the measured cycle, but the results presented in the summary above were not adjusted for this occurrence. All of the tests here were conducted with California Phase-II fuel (see Appendix C), at Toyota's request, and represent calculated volumetric fuel economies unadjusted in the manner currently used for gasoline-fueled certification vehicles.

I.   Introduction

The oil price shock experienced by the global marketplace in the mid-1970's had a profound effect on automobile design, toward models of increasing fuel efficiency. This experience was reinforced by the adoption in the United States of Federal Average Fuel Economy Standards, which provided requirements for automobile manufacturer sales fleet fuel economy. Federal and state clean-air regulations also required automakers to respond with automobiles that emitted lower levels of tailpipe hydrocarbons, carbon monoxide, and oxides of nitrogen.

Recently, concern has been raised in the scientific community and the public at large about climate change caused by the increased use of fossil fuels. In the United States, the use of fossil fuels for transportation purposes is a major source of carbon dioxide (CO_2) emissions. CO_2 is recognized by most of the scientific community as a "greenhouse effect" gas, promoting global warming. Improvements in new vehicle fuel economy have been leveling off in the United States, consistent with the fact that the fuel economy standards have remained constant. In addition, as domestic crude oil stocks become economically less profitable to extract, U.S. petroleum needs are being satisfied by relatively less expensive foreign source oil. This foreign source oil is a major concern with respect to a United States foreign trade deficit with the rest of the world.

Government and industry have responded to these environmental and trade concerns with a Presidential initiative, the "Partnership for a New Generation of Vehicles" (PNGV). PNGV is a joint Federal government/private industry effort which has as one goal the design and production of prototype vehicles with three times the fuel economy of 1993 baseline vehicles. These prototypes must be similar in load carrying capacity and performance to "baseline" sedan vehicles, such as the 1993 Chrysler Concorde, Chevrolet Lumina, or Ford Taurus vehicles. They must also meet Federal safety and emission standards in their year of introduction. Foreign automakers are also researching and designing automobiles that increase fuel efficiency and yet reduce regulated emissions to levels that are below those of comparable vehicles today.[1]

One near-term option for a relatively fuel efficient vehicle is a so-called "hybrid" powerplant vehicle. Hybrids typically make use of two powerplants, for example, a "conventional" internal combustion engine and an "unconventional" powerplant such as an electric motor system or flywheel energy storage system. The "unconventional" powerplants drive the vehicle during design-selected driving modes and may be designed to regenerate braking energy normally dissipated as heat. The "conventional" internal combustion engine may supplement, or recharge, the unconventional powerplant, and the engine may funnel its motive force either to the drive wheels directly through a common system with the unconventional powerplant, or possibly through a combination of both. Internal combustion engine displacement, output, "unconventional" powerplant characteristics, modes of operation, etc. are determined by the system designers to optimize the characteristics of the powerplants considered.

Toyota Motor Corporation recently announced the development of the Toyota Hybrid System (THS).[2] This hybrid vehicle makes use of an internal combustion engine, optimized for efficiency, a high-power battery, and an electric motor/generator (see vehicle description below). This vehicle has been in production in Japan since December 1997.

EPA made a request to Toyota Motor Corporation for a Toyota Hybrid System for evaluation at EPA's National Vehicle and Fuel Emissions Laboratory. Toyota responded favorably to this request

2

on February 3, 1998[3] and supplied EPA with a Prius hybrid vehicle on April 23, 1998. According to Toyota, the vehicle loaned to EPA by Toyota is representative of the Japanese production configuration and was not designed to meet the U.S. emission standards. This vehicle was evaluated over several different driving cycles and test conditions, and the results from this testing are presented and discussed in this report.

II. Description of Test Vehicle/Powerplants

A. Vehicle

The THS uses a 4-door Toyota Prius vehicle, with a curb weight of 2783 lbs with 100-percent fuel fill (Figures 1, 2, and 3, below). At Toyota's request, the vehicle was tested at 3000-lb test weight. A complete description of the test vehicle is provided in Appendix A.

Figure 1
Toyota Prius Hybrid Electric Vehicle

Figure 2
Toyota Prius THS - View of Vehicle Trunk

Figure 3
Toyota Prius THS - Engine Compartment

B.   Internal Combustion Engine

According to Toyota, the gasoline engine employed in this vehicle is specific to the THS and is not used currently with any other Toyota vehicle. The basic design is a 16-valve, 1.5-liter displacement, in-line 4-cylinder engine, with the head and block both constructed of aluminum. The combustion chamber is a compact pentroof design, employing a slanted squish area. The engine is mounted transversely, with a slight cant to the rear (Figure 3). An underfloor catalyst is placed in close proximity to the exhaust manifold.

The engine employs Toyota Variable Valve Timing with Intelligence (VVT-i). This system varies valve timing through the means of electronic control of an oil control valve, which in turn controls oil pressure to hydraulically actuate the VVT system pulley. The range of timing employed by the VVT-i in the THS is 40°.

The engine upper speed limit is 4000 rpm, and it operates through a generally narrow speed range. The operating cycle employed is a modified Atkinson cycle, with an expansion ratio of 13.5:1. Effective compression ratio is about 9:1, and late intake valve closure is employed. The engine produces 58 horsepower at 4000 rpm. Details are given in Appendix B, with further details available from the Toyota Motor Corporation.

C.   Electrical Propulsion System

The electrical drive system employs a permanent magnet electric motor, a generator, an inverter, and a nickel/metal-hydride battery pack. The motor itself acts as a generator during deceleration or braking, to convert the kinetic energy usually dissipated as heat in the friction brakes into electricity to recharge the battery. Detailed specifications are available from the Toyota Motor Corporation.

D.   Vehicle Operating Strategy

The THS utilizes a unique power "splitting" device that permits part of the internal combustion engine output to be applied to the wheels directly, while a portion of the output is applied to the generator, to the electric motor, and then to the wheels. Because of this "split," the Prius powertrain functions in a slightly different manner than a "conventional" parallel hybrid powertrain might be expected to function. A brief description of the THS powertrain function over typical driving modes is provided below.

The driving modes and strategies described below are summarized from the Toyota promotional literature.[1] EPA has not verified whether the vehicle drives in the manner prescribed here. This information is presented for informative purposes only.

Startup/Light Load: Toyota claims that the nickel hydride battery, providing power through the motor, runs the vehicle at startup and at light load.

Normal Driving: During "normal driving," the power splitting planetary geartrain is adjusted to divide the engine's output into two paths, one to drive the wheels directly and the second to drive the generator to produce electricity for the motor and/or charge the battery. The motor then can provide additional driving force to the wheels. The electronic control unit controls the distribution of power to the two separate driving force paths for maximum efficiency.

Deceleration/Braking: During deceleration, the inertia of the vehicle turns the motor, which then acts as a generator to recharge the battery.

Battery Charging: The electronic control unit signals the charging unit to maintain a near constant charge in the battery pack.

Full-Throttle Acceleration: During full-throttle acceleration or under heavy load, the motor is assisted by the battery so engine power and battery power are both used to drive the vehicle.

III. Test Facilities and Analytical Methods

EPA testing was conducted on dynamometer #2 of Site #1, Light-Duty Vehicle Test Site, at the EPA National Vehicle and Fuel Emissions Laboratory. The dynamometer used was a Horiba Electric Dynamometer, Model CDC-900, incorporating a single 48-inch roll, and capable of continuous power absorption from 0-125 hp at 65-mph conditions. The power exchange unit is an AC induction motor/generator. A Philco-Ford constant volume sampler, with blower set at 350 cfm was used. Hydrocarbon emissions were measured with a Beckman Model 400 flame ionization detector. Methane emissions were measured with a Bendix 8205 methane analyzer. CO and CO_2 were measured with Horiba AIA-23 infrared analyzers. NOx emissions were measured by chemiluminescent method with a Beckman 941-A analyzer.

EPA was provided by Toyota with a Hioki Model 3167 AC/DC Clamp-on Power Hi-Tester meter for use in quantifying the charging/discharging of the vehicle battery pack over a test mode. This meter provided an integrated measure of current flow and time to determine the net charge/discharge of the battery through the vehicle power management system during a test mode. This measure was given in amp-hours and is presented as "net" amp-hours in the data below (charge versus discharge). The sign convention used here is negative for net charging of the battery pack by the engine, and positive for net discharge of the battery through the motor to the wheels. Toyota provided EPA later in the evaluation with a Toyota Techno S2000 engine-scanning tool which could calculate an approximation to the state of charge of the battery pack (see discussion in IV, below). Toyota stated to EPA that the S2000 meter provides an index of SOC used internally by THS. Some testing was conducted utilizing SOC approximations before and after test modes.

IV. Prius Test Issues

The Toyota Prius hybrid (THS) system is currently offered for sale to the general public in Japan but is not sold in the United States. The California Air Resources Board has published a draft test procedure for emissions certification of new hybrid electric vehicles in the state of California. EPA has not promulgated test procedures for Federal emissions and fuel economy testing of hybrid vehicles.

Because of the nature of the hybrid electric powerplant, the power management system and hence, the emissions and fuel economy profile, of a hybrid vehicle may be considerably different than a vehicle equipped with a single internal combustion engine. Testing issues, because of these powerplant/management differences, may be raised in the interest of test-to-test variation, fairness, data measurement, significance, and safety. Some of these issues are discussed below.

The following terminology is used in this report to describe the battery conditions of the test vehicle:

State of Charge (SOC): If a battery's maximum charge capacity can be expressed in amp·hours, then the state of charge (SOC) is the percentage of that maximum amp-hour value remaining in the battery. SOC depends on many variables, and determining SOC is quite difficult. At present, there is not a universally accepted method or instrument for determining SOC from batteries.

Since one of the goals of testing hybrids is to either (1) have the state of charge of the energy storage system be the same at the beginning and the end of the test or (2) be able to adjust the results for any difference, measuring the energy storage system's status--the battery's state of charge in this case--is a critical test procedure issue.

Net Amp·Hours (NA·h): Net amp·hours represent the integrated result of the current into and out of the battery over a given time period. In order to measure NA·h, EPA utilized a meter provided by Toyota, a Hioki 3167 meter. Values determined using this meter are reported as net amp·hours in the test and the tables in this report.

Charge Index (CI): This index is used by the control system of the Toyota THS system. It is a calculated value which represents an approximation to the SOC of the battery. This index was measured by use of a scan tool, S2000, provided to EPA by Toyota.

It can be seen that both NA·h and CI are indicators of the battery's status and thus may be related to the battery's SOC.

Using Net Amp·Hours as a Surrogate for State of Charge

When Net amp·hours are used to characterize the status of the battery, consideration must be given to the voltage associated with discharging and charging the battery.

When current is being drawn from a battery, the voltage drops from the no-load (open circuit) voltage. Figure 4 shows discharging battery voltage versus percent- depth of discharge for a nickel metal hydride battery--the same type of battery as the one in the Prius test vehicle. The data are from GM Ovonic. The voltage at 90-amp discharge is less than the voltage at lower currents.

When a battery is being charged, the voltage generally exceeds the open circuit voltage. Therefore, it is possible that, for equal amp·hours in and out of the battery, the input and output power may not be the same. Therefore, using a criteria of Net amp·hours = zero may be slightly conservative in ensuring that the battery's status is the same before and after a test or a portion of a test.

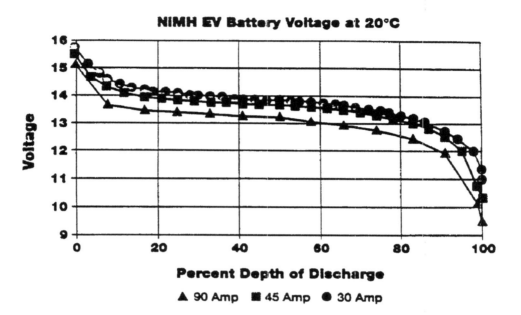

Figure 4
Discharging Battery Voltage Versus Level of Discharge
Nickel-Metal Hydride Battery

Maintenance Mode for Dynamometer Driving

It was necessary to invoke a "maintenance" mode of operation to permit dynamometer testing of the Prius THS. The Prius THS is equipped with a traction control system which would be activated when a significant difference between the front drive wheel and the rear wheel speeds is noticed. To allow testing on the EPA single-roll dynamometer, this "maintenance" mode was invoked by a series of accelerator and transmission position changes. According to Toyota, when the vehicle is in "maintenance mode" and when the gear shift selector is placed in the "drive" position, the traction control mode is disabled, and remaining vehicle operations are the same as the actual road driving mode. EPA did not perform any over-the-road tests of the Prius vehicle.

Manufacturer-Supplied Metering Equipment: Toyota supplied EPA with a directional current measurement (Hioki 3167) meter to determine net battery-pack charging/discharging over a driving mode or period of time.

Toyota also supplied EPA with a meter that Toyota claimed could be used to provide an internally used index of state of charge. (See Test Facilities section above.) Any equipment used to measure important parameters probably should be evaluated by EPA and/or by another independent group such as NIST with respect to performance, accuracy, and reliability. Although EPA made use of this manufacturer-supplied equipment during this evaluation in the interest of timeliness, EPA did not perform a separate evaluation of either instrument.

Effect of Preconditioning on Hybrid Electric Vehicles

The mpg of a test vehicle may be affected by the preconditioning, i.e., how the vehicle was operated prior to the test results being measured. Most prior operation considerations in the past have been related to vehicle thermal effects, primarily the degree to which the engine and emission control system in the vehicle have warmed up. For example, a cold-start test phase and a hot-start test phase are included in the standard emission test sequence.

In addition, current test protocols typically provide for operating a vehicle the day before the test on a specified urban driving cycle prior to the pre cold-start soak period.

Since the Prius is equipped with a gasoline-fueled spark engine, it was expected that there would be some sensitivity of the results to preconditioning based on engine and emission thermal characteristics. What was not known before the test program was run was the degree to which the emissions and fuel economy results of the Prius would be affected by its hybrid propulsion system, especially by the status of its battery.

Preconditioning Cars Equipped with Big Batteries: When a battery isn't being used, it loses charge. Conventional vehicles do have starting, lighting, and ignition (SLI) batteries, but their self-discharge has never been an issue for emission and fuel economy testing as far as preconditioning goes.

For some cars equipped with a hybrid electric propulsion system utilizing a battery big enough to provide traction power, the preconditioning issue may need to be re-examined. Figure 5 shows a battery self-discharge curve for a nickel-metal hydride battery. For a 20°C temperature, this battery loses about 1.3 percent of its charge per day. It should be noted that the data are from a nickel-metal hydride battery that is not the same as the nickel-metal hydride battery in the Toyota Prius.

Figure 5
Nickel-Metal Hydride Battery Self Discharge

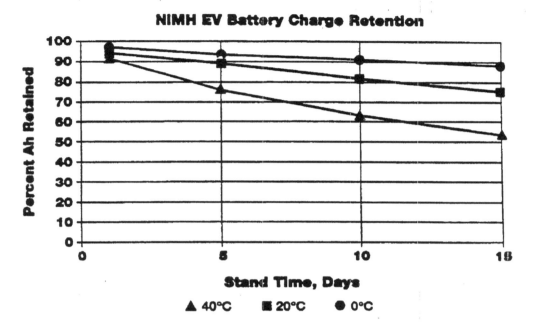

NIMH EV Battery Charge Retention

▲ 40°C   ■ 20°C   ● 0°C

Stand Time, Days

If one thinks of the battery as a fuel tank, a 1.3-percent loss per day is like a conventional vehicle with a 20-gallon fuel tank leaking a little more than a quart of fuel per day. The maximum power capacity of the THS battery back is 1.8kW·hr, however, which Toyota claims is equivalent to only 0.238 gallons of gasoline. In this example, therefore, a 1.3-percent discharge per day would be equivalent to about 0.003 gallons of gasoline per day.

Two Wheels on the Dyno versus Four Wheels on the Road: This issue has always been of concern to EPA since vehicles have been tested on chassis dynamometers. For hybrids with regenerative braking, the issue is more complicated. Consider the example of a vehicle like the Prius. It has front-wheel drive, and the front wheels are used for regenerative braking. Conventional friction brakes provide the braking for the rear wheels. In over the road driving, the percent of power consumed by the brakes is split between the front brakes and the rear brakes. According to Toyota, for the THS Prius, for normal braking conditions over LA-4 and HFET test schedules, the braking distribution is 90-95 percent to the drive axle. As a hypothetical example, say the front brakes provide 75 percent of the braking and the rear brakes the balance, 25 percent. When the vehicle is put on a single-roll chassis dynamometer, the front wheels drive, and the rear wheels do not move at all. If the vehicle is equipped with an antilock braking system and/or a traction control system, the system must be defeated, which was done for this testing.

On the dynamometer, the vehicle's front wheels provide 100 percent of the traction--like they do on the road--and 100 percent of the braking--which is not what happens on the road.

The potential problem with hybrid vehicle testing is with the representativeness of the regenerative braking on the dynamometer. Consider the previous example of 75%/25% road braking. If the front-wheel regenerative braking takes some fraction of the braking energy over the road, for example, say it is one-third, then a comparison of the over-the-road to chassis dynamometer braking energy distribution is shown in Table 1.

Given the example in Table 1, the amount of energy available for recharging on the dynamometer may be too high compared to what actually happens on the road, and it could be conjectured that the resulting mpg from the chassis dynamometer will be inappropriately high.

Table 1

Hypothetical Hybrid Vehicle		
	Braking Energy	
Braking Type	Over the Road	Chassis Dynamometer
Front Wheels Regeneration	25%	33%
Front Wheels Dissipative	50%	67%
Rear Wheels Dissipative	25%	0%
Total	100%	100%

Resolving this potential problem is beyond the scope of this report. Utilization of a chassis dynamometer configuration which exercises all the vehicle's wheels or special programming of a single-roll electric dynamometer's power absorption characteristics are two concepts that might be worthwhile to investigate.

Safety Considerations: Any hybrid vehicle will have an energy storage system that stores energy that can be rapidly discharged and recharged. When test vehicles are brought into a laboratory such as EPA's for testing, modifications are made to them to allow efficient testing, so some work is done on the test cars by test personnel. For hybrid vehicles, it is likely that, in the future, developers of hybrid propulsion systems should include information about possible hazards for people that work on the cars so accidents do not occur. For example, the Prius vehicle's battery pack is rated at 288 volts--a voltage high enough to be treated with care as it exceeds the voltage value usually considered to be potentially lethal.

V. Test Procedure

The testing described here was not conducted for purposes of emissions certification or the determination of official fuel economy values. The goal of this test program was to characterize the emissions, fuel economy, and (limited) performance of the THS over a variety of driving cycles and conditions of interest to EPA. In addition, there is no current Federal test procedure for the emissions certification of hybrid electric vehicles. EPA therefore tested the vehicle in a manner that would collect data of interest to a number of different audience groups.

Two test sequences, used in the THS evaluation here, are described in Figures 6 and 7. Figure 6 describes a 4-bag FTP test, preceded by a preconditioning drive over the LA-4 sequence and followed by a warm-up and measured Highway Fuel Economy Test (HFET) sequence. This entire test sequence is hereafter referred to as "Test Sequence 1" in this report. The second test sequence described in Figure 7 is hereafter referred to as "Test Sequence 2." Test Sequence 2 differs from Sequence 1 by designating the final vehicle drive on the day preceding a Sequence 2 test day as the preconditioning, regardless of the cycle driven, and by the 4-bag FTP being followed by a single, measured HFET. For all testing described as Sequence 1 or Sequence 2, below, the preconditioning drive between the second LA-4 and the HFET sequences was not conducted because the delay in all cases was less than 10 minutes. Tests were also conducted over the US06 and SC03 driving schedules; these tests are described in detail in separate subsections of Discussion of Test Results, below.

Performance testing, limited to 0-60 mph acceleration testing on the chassis dynamometer, was conducted. The mode of deceleration after the acceleration affected the charging of the battery. "Hard" and "medium" braking, determined by length of braking time from 62-63 mph to stopped conditions, with the gearshift selector in drive, caused the regenerative braking system to recharge the battery pack. "Coasting down" the vehicle, from 62-63 mph to 5 mph, braking thereafter to stop, recharged the vehicle during deceleration to a lesser degree than braking during the entire deceleration. Engaging the "neutral" position on the gear-shift selector, rather than the "drive" position, disengaged the engine and regenerative braking systems from the battery-charging circuit. This action was taken to discharge the battery; Toyota cautions against engaging the neutral position during actual driving for safety reasons. The resulting state of charge of the battery, following such testing, influenced successive acceleration tests. This testing is described further in the Discussion of Test Results, below.

Figure 6
Test Sequence Number 1

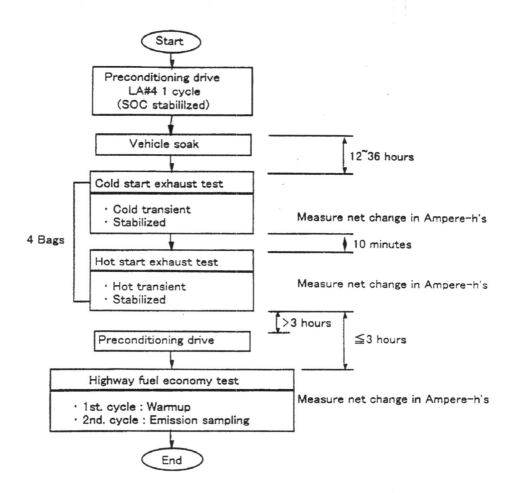

Figure 7
Test Sequence Number 2

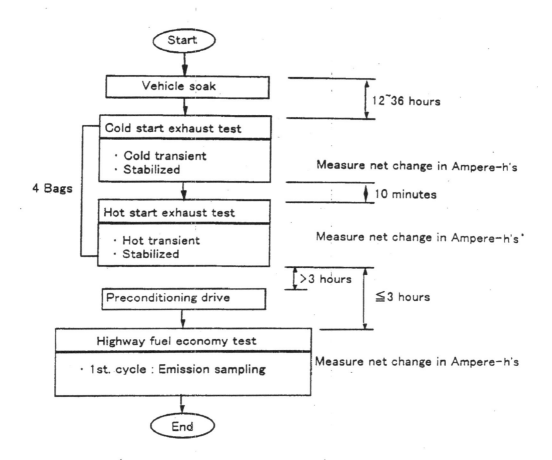

Tests were conducted at 10, 20, 30, 40, and 50 mph "steady-state" conditions. With a vehicle operated with an internal-combustion-engine-only powerplant, the vehicle is normally driven at the desired vehicle speed conditions until certain parameters, such as coolant temperature, engine oil temperature, etc. reach relatively steady-state conditions prior to emissions sampling. Because of the nature of the THS powerplants (the variance of the operation of the charging system and engine operation possibly related to state of battery charge), it was uncertain to EPA when "steady-state" conditions might be reached. It is important to note, therefore, that "steady-state" as referred to in this section, does not reflect battery condition. We conducted these "steady-state" tests in a manner consistent with steady-state testing of a conventional powerplant-only vehicle. The test results are referred to as steady-state test results, but the battery state of charge, particularly at 10-mph conditions, may materially influence the test results. The vehicle was operated at 10-mph speed conditions for a length of time (approximately 5 minutes) immediately following a driving preparation over the LA-4 cycle. Emissions sampling at 10-mph conditions was then conducted over a 10-minute sample interval. The vehicle was then driven to the next highest (20 mph) speed test point, driven for a period of time, and then sampled. This procedure was used for all steady-state sample points. This testing is described in a separate section below.

Testing was also conducted over the Hybrid Vehicle Testing Procedure in SAE J1711 (draft), and the (draft) California Air Resources Board Hybrid Electric Vehicle Test Procedure.[4,5] This testing was conducted for purposes of familiarization only and not to simulate a certification process. The data from this testing is presented in separate test summaries apart from this report.

VI.   Discussion of Test Results

A.   Performance (0-60 mph Acceleration) Testing

The Prius THS was first tested at the EPA National Vehicle and Fuel Emissions Laboratory on March 24, 1998. The vehicle was driven over the LA-4 (Urban Dynamometer Driving Schedule) cycle in order to familiarize the driver with the operation of the vehicle. This LA-4 cycle was followed immediately by driving the Highway Fuel Economy Test Cycle, again for the purpose of driver familiarization.

Upon completion of this familiarization performance testing, involving acceleration tests from 0 miles/hour (mph) (vehicle stop) to 60 mph was conducted. This testing was conducted, not only to obtain 0-60 mph test data but to determine the sensitivity of the vehicle's performance under hard acceleration conditions to the state of charge of the battery. (Per the discussion of vehicle driving strategies above, the THS electronic control unit requires electric motor power in addition to the mechanical power of the internal combustion engine at wide open throttle for maximum power at the drive wheels.)

Table 2 presents the results of 0-60 mph testing conducted on March 24, 1998. The testing was conducted by putting the foot accelerator pedal to the floor at start and releasing the accelerator at 62-65 mph conditions; 0-60 mph times were determined by analysis of the driver's trace of the acceleration. "Braking conditions" with 20 or 30 seconds refers to the time of braking, from start immediately following release of the accelerator, to 0 mph (vehicle stop). Twenty (20) seconds indicates 20 seconds of total deceleration time (braking during deceleration), much "harder" braking than the "30 seconds" conditions. This difference in braking conditions was done to determine the effect of regenerative braking on battery charging. "Coast/D" refers to coasting down the vehicle in Drive shift selector position. The vehicle was allowed to coast from the release of the accelerator pedal at 62-65 mph conditions to 5 mph, at which time moderate braking was applied to bring the vehicle to a stop. "Net Charge" refers to the net charging/discharging measured with the Hioki meter which occurred during the accel/decel cycle. (See Table 2 for conventions.)

During the three initial trials at "20 second" (harder) braking conditions, there was a net discharge from the battery over each accel/decel cycle. 0-60 mph times remained relatively constant over these three tests. Net battery discharge was much less during the fourth accel/decel, and the 0-60 mph time appeared to be affected by the three previous battery pack discharges. The 0-60 mph time rose considerably, to 17.3 seconds on the fifth accel/decel, and there was a slight net charge to the battery over this cycle. This charging appeared to influence performance, as the 0-60 mph time recorded on the sixth test was similar to those noted during the initial three accelerations.

19

Table 2

	Toyota Prius HEV 0-60 mph Acceleration Testing, 3/24/98		
Test Number	Braking Conditions	0-60 mph Time (sec)	Net Charge (Amp·hrs)*
1	20 seconds	14.4	0.232
2	20 seconds	14.2	0.327
3	20 seconds	14.2	0.325
4	30 seconds	15.1	0/033
5	30 seconds	17.3	-0.073
6	30 seconds	14.2	0.055
7	Coast/D	14.9	0.319
8	Coast/D	18.9	0.170
9	Coast/D	20.1	0.055
10	20 seconds	22.1	-0.254
11	20 seconds	19.2	-0.182
12	20 seconds	17.3	-0.078

* Negative Net Charge refers to net charging of the battery over the cycle, while positive Net Charge refers to a net battery discharge.

The effect of regenerative braking on change in charging was noted during the coastdown in drive mode. In the "maintenance mode" used during testing of the THS, the engine can charge the battery during decelerations, when the gear shift selector is placed in "drive," independently from the charging done through regenerative braking. During the first "coastdown in drive" (seventh accel/decel cycle) a substantial net discharge from the battery was noted. The effect of eliminating regenerative braking during the deceleration phase can be noted in the next three successive tests, with 0-60 mph times rising to a high of 22.1 seconds in test number 10. At this point, braking (hard) during deceleration was reintroduced, and 0-60 mph times began to fall, as net charging of the battery occurred during the accel/decel phase. The effect of reintroduction of regenerative braking led to a 0-60 mph time of 17.3 seconds after two cycles.

Table 3 refers to 0-60 mph testing conducted on April 6, 1998. "Coast/N" refers to coasting down from the end of the acceleration by putting the gear shift selector into "neutral" position, coasting down to 5-mph conditions, and braking to a full stop thereafter. This mode of operation is not recommended by Toyota but was performed to simulate extreme conditions of battery discharge.

Table 3

Toyota Prius HEV 0-60 mph Testing, 4/6/98			
Test Number	Braking Conditions	0-60 mph (sec)	Net Charge (Amp·hrs) *
1	20 seconds	14.1	.314
2	20 seconds	14.1	.302
3	20 seconds	14.2	.297
4	30 seconds	14.1	.305
5	30 seconds	14.1	.303
6	30 seconds	13.9	.299
7	Coast/N	14.0	.298
8	Coast/N	15.3	.222
9	Coast/N	18.0	.117
10	Coast/N	18.9	.065
11	Coast/N	19.1	.054
12	Coast/N	19.4	.040
13	Coast/N	19.6	.042
14	Coast/N	19.5	.039

* "Net Charge" here refers to the net charge (positive values meaning net battery discharge and negative values meaning charging of the battery pack) over the acceleration phase only, not to include the deceleration.

The "hard" versus "medium" braking did not seem to influence the 0-60 mph acceleration times noted in this testing. Coasting down in neutral prevented regenerative braking and engine recharge from charging the battery during the deceleration, as "neutral" position decoupled both the engine and regenerative braking from the charging circuit. Coasting down in neutral was done to quickly discharge the vehicle battery pack; Toyota recommends against engaging the neutral position during actual driving for safety reasons. The net discharge of the battery gradually lessened as these tests were repeated. Figure 8 presents the decreasing net discharge from the battery per acceleration graphed against 0-60 mph acceleration time. A 0-60 mph acceleration time in excess of 19 seconds is indicated when the discharge of the battery during acceleration is minimized, i.e., engine-only operation. Therefore, it seems that the acceleration time of this vehicle is influenced by the state of charge of the battery and ranges from about 14 seconds to about 20 seconds, depending on the state of charge.

Figure 8
0-60 mph Acceleration Time versus Battery Discharge

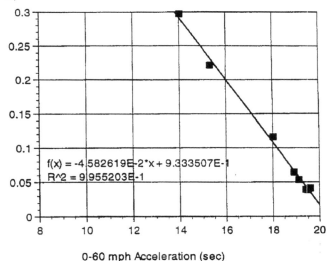

B. Testing Over Consecutive HFET Sequences

On two separate occasions, EPA conducted tests over successive HFET cycles with the THS. This testing was conducted to determine whether a relationship between battery charge/discharge over the HFET and measured fuel economy could be determined. The first sequence consisted of five consecutive HFET's; data from this test is presented below in Table 4.

Table 4

Toyota Prius THS Five Consecutive Tests Over HFET Cycle							
Test No.	FID HC	NMHCE	CO	NO$_x$	CO$_2$	Fuel Economy	Net Charge
	g/mi	g/mi	g/mi	g/mi	g/mi	MPG	Amp·hrs*
1	0.01	0.01	0.4	0.05	183	47.00	-0.871
2	0.01	0.01	0.3	0.06	163	52.80	-0.114
3	0.02	0.01	0.3	0.07	162	53.02	0.049
4	0.02	0.02	0.3	0.05	163	52.67	-0.099
5	0.03	0.02	0.3	0.06	161	53.30	-0.063

* Negative values indicate net charging of the battery pack over the test cycle; positive values indicate net discharge of the battery pack.

Prior to the first HFET in Table 4, a number of 0-60 mph acceleration tests were conducted (See A, above). The battery discharging which occurred during these acceleration tests influenced the first test substantially. The following tests recorded fuel economies in excess of 52 mpg for relatively similar battery charge/discharge levels. The highest HFET cycle fuel economy recorded here, 53.30 mpg, occurred with a slight net battery charging over the test cycle.

23

Figure 9, below, is a simultaneous plot of fuel economy versus net battery charging/discharging measured in net amp-hours. The straight line least squares method relationship shown here gives a zero net battery charge/discharge value of 53.32 mpg.

Figure 9
Consecutive Tests Over The HFET Cycle
Fuel Economy versus Net Battery Charge/Discharge
(Data From Table 4)

Fuel Economy [MPG]

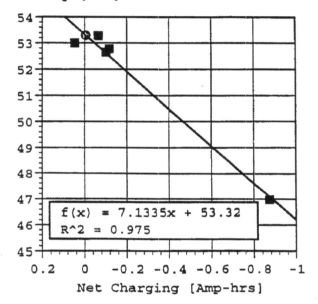

Net Charging [Amp-hrs]

O = MPG at Zero Net Charging

Table 5, below, presents the results of testing over 12 consecutively conducted HFET's with the THS. A problem with the programming of the Hioki 3167 meter prevented the reading of battery charge/discharge over the first four HFET's here. The test results from the first test described in Table 5 were influenced by the deep discharge of the vehicle battery pack prior to the commencement of testing. The remaining tests had fuel economy and net charge/discharge values not dissimilar to those recorded with the latter four tests referred to in Table 4.

Table 5

Toyota Prius THS							
Twelve Consecutively Conducted Tests Over HFET Cycle							
Test No.	FID HC	NMHCE	CO	NO$_x$	CO$_2$	Fuel Economy	Net Charge*
	g/mi	g/mi	g/mi	g/mi	g/mi	MPG	Amp·hrs
1	0.13	0.12	0.7	0.07	186	46.08	NA
2	0.04	0.03	0.3	0.07	159	53.92	NA
3	0.04	0.04	0.3	0.06	159	54.01	NA
4	0.04	0.04	0.3	0.05	160	53.82	NA
5	0.04	0.04	0.3	0.05	157	54.65	0.055
6	0.04	0.03	0.3	0.06	160	53.80	−0.016
7	0.05	0.04	0.3	0.08	165	52.27	−0.034
8	0.04	0.03	0.3	0.06	159	54.17	0.018
9	0.04	0.03	0.3	0.06	160	53.84	−0.023
10	0.04	0.04	0.3	0.06	160	53.85	−0.024
11	0.04	0.03	0.3	0.06	159	54.25	−0.029
12	0.04	0.03	0.3	0.06	160	53.65	0.064

*Negative values relate to net battery-pack charging over the test cycle; positive values relate to net battery-pack discharge over the cycle.

Figure 10 is a least squares linear relationship between net charge/discharge and fuel economy for the last eight tests in Table 5. Greater scatter in the data appears to be indicated, but this is a function somewhat of the narrow range of charge/discharge conditions experienced in the latter eight tests. The "zero net charge/discharge" fuel economy indicated by Figure 10 for this data is 53.80 mpg, somewhat similar to the 53.32 mpg referred to in Figure 9.

Figure 10
Consecutive Tests Over the HFET Cycle
Fuel Economy versus Net Battery Charge/Discharge
(Data From Table 5)

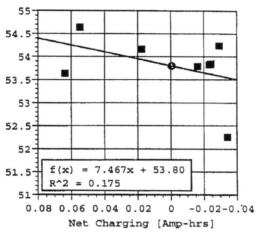

O = MPG at Zero Net Charging

C.   Combined City/Highway Emissions/Fuel Economy Testing

The Prius THS was evaluated over two test conventions
utilizing a modified Federal test procedure (FTP) and Highway
Fuel Economy Test (HFET) cycle sequence. (See Test Procedure,
Section V, above). Test Sequence No. 1 consists of an LA-4
vehicle conditioning drive, followed the next day with a 4-Bag
FTP (cold start and hot start Urban Dynamometer Driving Schedule
tests), and two HFET cycles (conditioning and measured). Test
Sequence No. 2 eliminated the preconditioning HFET and the need
to precondition over the LA-4 during the preview test day. All
testing was conducted using California Phase II Reformulated
Gasoline (see Appendix C) at the request of Toyota. Dynamometer
coefficients and suggested vehicle test weight was supplied by
Toyota, with details provided in Appendix A.

Table 6, below, presents the results of testing over the 4-Bag FTP cycles. Integrated, cumulative battery charging, measured immediately before and after each test, is also provided. The difference between these data points, or net charging/discharge of the battery pack over the test cycle, is also presented. The tests conducted on April 3, April 23 and 24, 1998, were conducted to the Test Sequence No. 1 procedure, utilizing a conditioning HFET as well as a "measured" HFET, following the 4-Bag FTP. EPA measured emissions during both HFET's therefore enabling the first HFET to be used to simulate the Test Sequence No. 2 cycle, referred to above. HFET results using the Test Sequence No. 2 procedure are given in the following table, Table 7.

Table 6

Toyota Prius THS "4-Bag FTP" Test Cycle							
Test Date	FID HC	NMHC E	CO	NO_x	CO_2	Fuel Economy	Net Charge*
	g/mi	g/mi	g/mi	g/mi	g/mi	MPG	Amp·hrs
03/25/98	0.06	0.06	0.5	0.04	178	48.24	NA
03/27/98	0.08	0.07	0.4	0.05	175	49.07	0.181
03/28/98	0.07	0.06	0.5	0.05	181	47.43	0.203
03/31/87	0.07	0.06	0.6	0.05	181	47.40	−0.344
04/01/98	0.06	0.06	0.4	0.05	173	49.65	0.166
04/02/98	0.06	0.05	0.4	0.06	172	49.94	0.184
04/03/98	0.06	0.06	0.4	0.05	181	47.48	−0.285
04/23/98	0.06	0.05	0.4	0.07	182	47.21	−0.132
04/24/98	0.06	0.05	0.4	0.05	174	49.36	−0.038

* Negative values relate to net battery-pack charging over the test cycle; positive values relate to net battery-pack discharge over the cycle.

Table 7

Toyota Prius THS HFET Test Results First HFET After the Four-Bag Test Used							
Test Date	FID HC	NMHCE	CO	NO$_x$	CO$_2$	Fuel Economy	Net Charge*
	g/mi	g/mi	g/mi	g/mi	g/mi	MPG	Amp·hrs
03/25/98	0.03	0.03	0.3	0.06	176	48.76	-0.462
03/27/98	0.04	0.03	0.3	0.05	173	49.71	NA
03/28/98	0.05	0.04	0.4	0.04	176	48.75	NA
03/31/98	0.04	0.04	0.3	0.05	174	49.48	-0.370
04/01/98	0.04	0.04	0.3	0.04	174	49.41	-0.409
04/02/98	0.04	0.04	0.4	0.04	175	49.03	-0.412
04/03/98	0.04	0.04	0.3	0.06	170	48.65	-0.488
04/23/98	0.01	0.01	0.2	0.06	180	47.96	-0.370
04/24/98	0.02	0.02	0.2	0.04	177	48.62	-0.388

* Negative values relate to net battery-pack charging over the test cycle; positive values relate to net battery-pack discharge over the cycle.

Emissions of hydrocarbons, carbon monoxide, and oxides of nitrogen over the a 4-Bag FTP exhibit little test-to-test variability. These emission levels are low with respect to current model year Federal certification standards, particularly the levels of oxides of nitrogen. It should be noted that some of these tests have positive, or net battery discharge, levels over the entire 4-Bag FTP. A net battery discharge may indicate that more work was done by the battery/motor system to drive the vehicle over the test cycle than for a similar test with net battery charging (from the internal combustion engine). For similar work at the drive wheels, a greater share or proportion of the work done by the battery/motor implies less work done by the internal combustion engine, with a net discharge of the battery pack. Some of the tests involve net charging, and others had net battery discharge noted over the 4-Bag FTP. For the charge/discharge levels noted here, there is not enough sensitivity exhibited to state conclusively a relation between emissions and charge/discharge. This is an area where further testing may be helpful. Fuel economy varied over a range of slightly less than 3 mpg, from 47.21 mpg to a high of 49.94 mpg. A discussion of calculated fuel economy versus charging over the test cycle is given later.

Little variation in emissions over the HFET following the 4-Bag FTP is exhibited in Table 7. The two tests with the lowest net charging of the battery noted here (-0.370 amp-hrs) had some of the highest and lowest calculated fuel economies over the HFET, 49.48 and 47.976 mpg, respectively.

Composite, or "55/45" fuel economy values are given below in Table 8. The second column presents composite emissions calculated in the manner normally used by EPA to calculate composite city/highway fuel economy. Slightly higher fuel economies appear to be associated with tests that had less total battery recharging noted over the entire test.

Table 8

Toyota Prius THS Composite City/Highway Fuel Economy Test Sequence No. 2		
Test Date	Composite Calculated Fuel Economy	Net Charge*
	MPG	Amp·hrs
03/25/98	48.47	NA
03/27/98	49.36	NA
03/28/98	48.02	NA
03/31/98	48.31	-0.714
04/01/98	49.54	-0.243
04/02/98	49.53	-0.228
04/03/98	48.00	-0.772
04/23/98	47.54	-0.502
04/24/98	49.02	-0.426

* Negative values relate to net battery-pack charging over the test cycle; positive values relate to net battery-pack discharge over the cycle.

D.   Testing Over Designated Test Sequence No. 1

The test sequence designated as No. 1 consisted of the 4-Bag FTP followed by two tests over the HFET cycle, a conditioning test and the "measured" test. Sequence No. 1 was evaluated four times, but EPA sampled both HFET's in order to facilitate a comparison between the sequences designated "1" and "2."

The 4-Bag FTP test results were presented earlier in Table 6, in the section discussing the Sequence No. 2 "test cycle," as the 4-Bag FTP's over Sequence No. 2 are inclusive of those over Sequence No. 1.   This data is given here in Table 9, to facilitate a later comparison.   HFET results from both the No. 2 and No. 1 sequences are given simultaneously in Table 10 for comparison.

Table 9

Toyota Prius THS Tests Over 4-Bag FTP Test Sequence No. 1							
Test Date	FID HC	NMHCE	CO	NO$_x$	CO$_2$	FE	Net Charge*
	g/mi	g/mi	g/mi	g/mi	g/mi	MPG	Amp-hrs
04/03/98	0.06	0.06	0.4	0.05	181	47.48	-0.285
04/17/98	0.05	0.04	0.4	0.05	177	48.57	-0.252
04/23/98	0.06	0.05	0.4	0.07	182	47.21	-0.132
04/24/98	0.06	0.05	0.4	0.05	174	49.36	-0.038

* Negative values relate to net battery-pack charging over the test cycle; positive values relate to net battery-pack discharge over the cycle.

We monitored manifold vacuum as an indicator on engine "on/off" condition during the LA-4.   (Toyota has stated that the engine shuts off during decelerations and at idle.) Approximately 27-31 engine starts were noted over the cold start LA-4 cycle.

Table 10

Test Date	FID HC*	NMHCE	CO	NOₓ	CO₂	FE	Net** Charge
	g/mi	g/mi	g/mi	g/mi	g/mi	g/mi	Amp-hrs

Toyota Prius TES
HFET Results--Test Sequence No. 1

Test Date	FID HC* g/mi	NMHCE g/mi	CO g/mi	NO_x g/mi	CO_2 g/mi	FE g/mi	Net** Charge Amp-hrs
04/03/98	0.04/ 0.04	0.04/ 0.04	0.3/ 0.3	0.05/ 0.06	177/ 164	48.65/ 52.60	-0.488/ -0.080
04/17/98	NA/ 0.01	NA/ 0.01	NA/ 0.2	NA/ 0.04	NA/ 166	NA/ 51.88	-0.444/ -0.052
04/23/98	0.01/ 0.01	0.01/ 0.01	0.2/ 0.2	0.06/ 0.05	180/ 167	47.96/ 51.45	-0.370/ -0.014
04/24/98	0.02/ 0.02	0.02/ 0.02	0.2/ 0.1	0.04/ 0.05	177/ 165	48.62/ 52.04	-0.338/ -0.097

* The first figure in each column relates to test results over the first
HFET following the 4-Bag FTP (Test Sequence No. 2) test; the second
figure in each column relates to test results over the second HFET
following the 4-Bag FTP (Test Sequence No. 1).
** Negative values relate to net battery-pack charging over the cycle;
positive values relate to net battery-pack discharge over the cycle.

The emission results, with the exception of CO_2, are
relatively similar for the sequence No. 2 HFET compared to Test
Sequence No. 1. The vehicle battery pack was charged
significantly more by the internal combustion engine over the
first HFET. CO_2 emissions increased, and hence fuel economy
decreased over the first HFET because of the additional charging
work done by the engine.

The difference in HFET fuel economy is approximately seven-
percent higher for the average of the second HFET versus the
first HFET.

These differences in highway fuel economy will carry over to
calculated composite (city and highway) fuel economy values.
Table 11 below presents calculated composite fuel economies for
the four tests above conducted with both Test Sequences No. 1 and
No. 2 procedures.

Table 11

Toyota Prius THS Composite MPG - Test Sequences No. 2 and No. 1 Procedures			
Test Date	City MPG	Highway MPG*	Composite MPG
04/03/98	47.48	48.65/52.60	48.00/49.66
04/17/98	48.57	NA/51.88	NA/50.01
04/23/98	47.21	47.96/51.45	47.54/49.03
04/24/98	49.36	48.62/52.04	49.02/50.53

* The first figure in the column refers to test results over the first
HFET following the 4-Bag FTP test (Test Sequence No. 2 procedure); the
second figure in each column refers to test results over the second
HFET following the 4-Bag FTP (Test Sequence No. 1 procedure).

The average composite fuel economy for the three tests
conducted with Test Sequence No. 2 was about 48.2 mpg,
approximately three-percent lower than the 49.8 mpg average over
the same tests with Test Sequence No. 1 procedure. This
difference is probably due in large part to the additional
charging of the THS battery pack during the first HFET conducted
following the 4-Bag FTP.

E.   Hot Start FTP Following Battery Discharge

A single 4-Bag FTP test was conducted with the THS following
the deep discharge of the battery pack. This test was conducted
to determine the effect on emissions and fuel economy of an
excursion or incident which would cause the battery pack to
discharge to a very low state of charge. Until the battery pack
charged to a "normal" level, this discharge would cause the
vehicle power management system to task the THS internal
combustion engine heavily, to include vehicle propulsion and
battery pack charging, over a given driving cycle.

EPA had determined that a demanding acceleration from stop,
followed by coasting down the vehicle with the gear selector in
"N" position, would discharge the battery. (A wide open throttle
acceleration from stop causes the THS power management system to
invoke battery-pack operation of the electric motor. Changing
the gear shift selector from "D" position to "N" disengages the
engine/battery and regenerative braking recharging systems in the
dynamometer driving mode used.) It should be noted that Toyota
cautions against using the neutral "gear shift" position during
actual driving for safety reasons.

A 0-60 mph wide open throttle acceleration from stop was performed on the vehicle, the driver removing his foot from the accelerator and engaging the "N" gear selector mode when the vehicle reached approximately 61 mph. The vehicle was allowed to coast to 5-mph conditions in "N" position, light braking was then used to bring the vehicle to full stop. The change in battery-pack charging/discharging during this acceleration was recorded (net discharge of battery pack occurred.), as well as 0-60 mph acceleration time, by means of a stopwatch. This "preparation" of the vehicle/battery pack was repeated until simultaneously, 1) 0-60 mph acceleration times stabilized, and 2) net battery discharge during acceleration decreased to nearly zero. At this point, EPA was satisfied that the THS power management system and battery pack had caused the pack to discharge to the lowest charge level possible with this preparation.

Table 12 presents Bag 1 (first 505 seconds of the LA04 cycle) emissions. The effect of deeper battery discharge is noticeable in higher hydrocarbon and NOx emissions, and lower fuel economy compared with the "normally" charged (conditioned over the LA-4 cycle the previous afternoon) battery pack test data. The large net charge indicated substantial battery charging during this mode, with respect to the "normally" charged battery tests.

Table 12

Toyota Prius Hybrid Vehicle LA-4 Test Cycle Test Following Battery-Pack Discharge							
Cold Start "Bag 1" Emissions/FE							
Test Conditions /Date**	FID HC	NMHCE	CO	NO$_x$	CO$_2$	FE	Net Charge*
	g/mi	g/mi	g/mi	g/mi	g/mi	MPG	Amp·hrs
Discharge	0.41	0.40	1.2	0.3	307	27.9	-1.577
03/31/98	0.25	0.23	1.4	0.1	254	33.6	-0.522
04/01/98	0.22	0.21	1.2	0.2	235	36.9	-0.154
04/02/98	0.20	0.19	0.8	0.1	228	37.5	-0.164

* Negative values relate to net battery-pack charging over the test cycle; positive values relate to net battery-pack discharge over the cycle.
** Dated tests denote "normally" charged battery pack prior to test.

Tables 13-15 present Bag 2 through Bag 4 data for the same tests. Emission levels and even fuel economy for the "deeply discharged" battery pack test do not differ greatly from the data added for comparison purposes. This may indicate relatively rapid battery recharging to manufacturer desired state of charge level following a substantial battery pack drain.

Table 13

Toyota Prius Hybrid Vehicle LA-4 Test Cycle Test Following Battery-Pack Discharge							
Stabilized "Bag 2" Emissions/FE							
Test Conditions /Date**	FID HC	NMHCE	CO	NO_x	CO_2	FE	Net Charge*
	g/mi	g/mi	g/mi	g/mi	g/mi	MPG	Amp·hrs
Discharge	0.01	0.01	0.1	0.05	130	66.3	−0.506
03/31/98	0.01	0.01	0.2	0.03	141	61.1	−0.332
04/01/98	0.01	0.01	0.1	0.04	133	65.0	−0.458
04/02/98	0.01	0.004	0.2	0.04	129	66.7	−0.433

* Negative values relate to net battery-pack charging over the test cycle; positive values relate to net battery-pack discharge over the cycle.
** Dated tests denote "normally" charged battery pack prior to test.

Table 14

Toyota Prius Hybrid Vehicle LA-4 Test Cycle Test Following Battery-Pack Discharge							
Hot Start "Bag 3" Emissions/FE							
Test Conditions/ Date**	FID HC	NMHCE	CO	NO_x	CO_2	FE	Net Charge*
	g/mi	g/mi	g/mi	g/mi	g/mi	MPG	Amp·hrs
Discharge	0.04	0.03	0.3	0.08	191	45.0	-0.273
03/31/98	0.05	0.04	0.6	0.06	198	43.3	-0.278
04/01/98	0.04	0.03	0.5	0.06	197	43.7	-0.347
04/02/98	0.05	0.04	0.6	0.07	192	44.6	-0.236

* Negative values relate to net battery-pack charging over the test cycle;
positive values relate to net battery-pack discharge over the cycle.
** Dated tests denote "normally" charged battery pack prior to test.

Table 15

Toyota Prius Hybrid Vehicle LA-4 Test Cycle Test Following Battery-Pack Discharge							
Stabilized "Bag 4" Emissions/FE							
Test Conditions /Date**	FID HC	NMHCE	CO	NO_x	CO_2	FE	Net Charge*
	g/mi	g/mi	g/mi	g/mi	g/mi	MPG	Amp·hrs
Discharge	0.01	0.01	0.2	0.04	136	63.5	-0.284
03/31/98	0.01	0.01	0.2	0.03	146	59.1	-0.119
04/01/98	0.01	0.004	0.1	0.04	139	61.9	-0.208
04/02/98	0.01	0.002	0.2	0.04	146	59.1	-0.151

* Negative values relate to net battery-pack charging over the test cycle;
positive values relate to net battery-pack discharge over the cycle.
** Dated tests denote "normally" charged battery pack prior to test.

Table 16 represents the total effect on fuel economy and emissions over the 4-bag FTP of the deep battery-pack discharge prior to testing. Total weighted hydrocarbons and NOx emission levels exceed those of the "normally preconditioned" battery-pack testing, though CO levels are still arguably as low as those from the comparison tests. Battery charging over the entire FTP cycle is much greater for the deeply discharged battery-pack test, but this is influenced by the high degree of recharging in Bag 1. Fuel economy is approximately 5 percent below the simple average of the "normally preconditioned" battery tests presented here.

Table 16

Toyota Prius Hybrid Vehicle LA-4 Test Cycle Test Following Battery-Pack Discharge							
Composite Emissions/Fuel Economy							
Test Conditions /Date**	FID HC	NMHCE	CO	NO_x	CO_2	FE	Net Charge*
	g/mi	g/mi	g/mi	g/mi	g/mi	MPG	Amp·hrs
Discharge	0.10	0.10	0.4	0.11	185	44.41	-1.060
03/31/98	0.07	0.06	0.6	0.05	181	47.40	-0.344
04/01/98	0.06	0.06	0.4	0.05	173	49.65	-0.166
04/02/98	0.06	0.05	0.4	0.06	172	49.94	-0.184

* Negative values relate to net battery-pack charging over the test cycle; positive values relate to net battery-pack discharge over the cycle.
** Dated tests denote "normally" charged battery pack prior to test.

F. Testing Over SC03 Driving Schedule

The SC03 test cycle is designed to measure emissions during ambient conditions when air conditioning use is likely. The test cell was conditioned to 95°F and 100 grains water/lb. of dry air. Test procedures for this 594-second test are given in the Code of Federal Regulations.[6] Note that the ambient conditions simulated are those which are conducive to formation of ozone in the atmosphere.

The EPA testing plan called for a sequence of four tests over the SC03 on the day of the evaluation, a preparation (no emissions measurement), followed by three consecutive tests with emissions measured. A 10-minute soak separated each SC03 test.

The "conditioning" and the first two SC03 (measured) tests were conducted without incident. Approximately 400 seconds into the third measured SC03 test, a fuel line hose in the top of the fuel tank (in the fuel sending unit assembly) became detached from its connection to the fuel sending unit. Fuel bubbled out of the tank through this opening, leaking over the tank and underside of the vehicle onto the floor of the test cell. The odor of fuel in the vehicle was immediately noted by the vehicle driver, and the test was halted. The fuel leak and the spilled fuel were addressed. A plastic clip which attached the fuel line to the top of the fuel sending unit had been previously removed by EPA to facilitate the drain of fuel from the vehicle tank through this opening. This clip had been replaced after the fuel drain was conducted (when the vehicle was initially accepted by EPA). The driver noted that this clip had "popped off" the hose/sending-unit fitting when the leak occurred.

The fuel line was replaced on the sending unit, and the attaching clip reinstalled. The vehicle was soaked again to test conditions, and the test sequence begun again with the "prep" SC03. During this test, the fuel line and the retainer clip disconnected from the fuel-sending unit. A fuel leak from the tank, similar to the above, then developed. The fuel leak was attended to, and the testing halted to better determine the cause of the fuel-fitting failures.

Toyota Technical Center representatives consulted with EPA to analyze the cause of the fuel-fitting failure. It was suggested by Toyota that the fitting retainer clip may have been designed to be used or "stretched" only once; therefore, re-use of this clip may not have been advisable. Toyota supplied EPA with another retainer clip (new), and this clip was used to secure the fuel line to the sending unit. Toyota and EPA jointly decided to suspend further testing over the SC03 cycle in the interest of Toyota making a more detailed determination at a later date of the cause of the failure. The original, "reused" retainer clip was returned to Toyota for analysis.

The issue of preparing hybrid vehicles for testing at vehicle laboratories is one that must be addressed in greater detail by EPA and the vehicle manufacturers in the future (see Testing Issues, above). Additional documentation will most certainly have to be supplied by the manufacturers concerning alternative modes of operation (if any) of the powerplants, detailed start and prep instructions, safety information concerning operation of the battery and electric motor, safety during off-vehicle charging (if necessary), etc.

The data from the first two tests over the SC03 test cycle (conducted without incident), together with charging information over the first (conditioning) SC03 cycle excursion, is presented below. This data is presented with limited comment; no comparatory data is given here. The calculated fuel economy figures are similar for both tests, and the net battery charges for both "measured" tests were similar in magnitude and sign (slight battery charge provided by engine).

The "conditioning" (no emissions measured) drive had a higher net charge to the battery than the following two tests over the SC03 cycle. During the afternoon prior to the day of the SC03 cycle testing, a number of 0-60 mph acceleration tests had been conducted. The vehicle was coasted down in the "drive" mode (no regenerative braking) during the decelerations following the 0-60 mph accelerations. Therefore, the state of charge of the hybrid electric battery pack may have been reduced prior to the conduct of the SC03 testing, helping to explain the relatively higher amount of charging noted during the "prep" SC03 driving cycle.

Table 17

	Toyota Prius HEV Testing Over SC03 ("Air Conditioner") Test Sequence						
Test No.	FID HC	NMHCE	CO	NO$_x$	CO$_2$	Net Charge*	FE
	g/mi	g/mi	g/mi	g/mi	g/mi	Amp·hrs	MPG
1	N/A	N/A	N/A	N/A	N/A	-0.407	N/A
2	0.04	0.04	0.4	0.02	258	-0.65	33.36
3	0.08	0.06	0.6	0.06	256	-0.51	33.57

* Negative values relate to net battery-pack charging over the test cycle; positive values relate to net battery-pack discharge over the cycle.

G.   Testing Over the US06 Test Cycle

The Federal US06 Driving Schedule is a high speed, "aggressive" schedule, involving some high accelerations. These driving modes may cause some vehicles to operate in an "open loop," or full power mode (with respect to air/fuel setpoints on a 3-way catalyst equipped vehicle.)

Six consecutive emission tests with the THS over the US06 cycle were conducted on a single day. The THS had been tested over the 4-bag FTP, followed by three tests over the HFET cycle, prior to the US06 testing. The vehicle was driven and tested over the US06 cycle three times in succession. Testing was then halted, and a number of 0-60 mph accelerations, followed by shift into neutral and braking to stop, were conducted. This action put the vehicle battery pack into a state of deeper discharge characterized by the appearance of a warning indicator on the vehicle video dashboard. With the vehicle battery in this state of discharge, the THS was tested over the US06 cycle again. Battery discharging in the same manner as above was again conducted, the US06 test repeated, and the discharge/test sequence repeated a third time, for a total of three tests in this mode. This "discharged battery" testing was conducted to determine the effect on emissions and fuel economy of driving the THS Prius over a demanding driving schedule with the battery package greatly discharged. Toyota notes that this condition of battery discharge would not be contemplated by their designers under normal driving conditions. Results from this testing are presented below in Table 18.

39

The CO_2 emission levels are an indication that the vehicle engine attempted to recharge the battery pack following the deeper discharge. Calculated fuel economy therefore decreased, approximately 11 percent from the level of the "normally" charged battery US06 tests. Emission levels, however, changed little as a result of the deeper battery discharge (a slight increase in CO emissions was noted).

In general, the vehicle driver noted a degradation in driving performance over the US06 following the battery deep discharge (compared to the "normally" charged battery). For example, the driver was not able to follow the driver's trace over one early, particularly demanding, acceleration during each of the deep discharge battery US06 tests. No effort is made here to quantify the THS performance or relate battery charge to the ability to follow the trace and time following start of test. It is noted, however, that performance over the US06 was related to the state of charge of the battery, for a "deeper" discharge of the battery pack prior to the start of the test.

Table 18

	HC	NMHCE	CO	CO_2	NO_x	Fuel Economy	Net Charge*
Toyota Prius HEV Consecutive Tests Over US06 Schedule							
Battery Mode	g/mi	g/mi	g/mi	g/mi	g/mi	MPG	Amp·hrs
"A"**	0.03	0.03	0.5	232	0.09	37.02	0.265
"A"	0.03	0.03	0.6	235	0.09	36.64	0.058
"A"	0.03	0.03	0.6	234	0.07	36.64	0.302
"B"***	0.03	0.03	0.7	267	0.09	32.19	-0.854
"B"	0.03	0.03	0.9	251	0.07	32.90	-0.554
"B"	0.04	0.03	0.7	260	0.09	33.05	-0.405

* Negative values relate to net battery-pack charging over the test cycle; positive values relate to net battery-pack discharge over the cycle.
** "A" denotes normally charged battery pack prior to first US06, then followed by two additional US06 tests in succession.
*** "B" denotes deep discharge of battery pack, evidenced by dashboard warning indicator, prior to test over US06 cycle.

H.   Testing Over Select Vehicle Steady-State Speed Modes

The THS was tested over several steady-state vehicle operating modes for emissions and fuel economy. The hybrid powerplant system must also be considered in the discussion of the results from this testing, however.

With a conventional vehicle, a desired vehicle speed is driven with a set of dynamometer load coefficients. Parameters such as coolant temperature, oil temperature, emissions, etc. are monitored until the tester is satisfied that steady-state operating conditions are present, and then emissions sampling is begun. With a hybrid electric vehicle, like the THS, the state of battery-pack charge may determine the apportionment of engine and motor operation of the drive wheels, battery recharging during vehicle operation, etc. Therefore, the operation of the internal combustion engine and electrical drive system might change during "steady-state" testing. It is important to note, therefore, that "steady-state" as referred to in this section, does not reflect battery condition. We conducted these "steady-state" tests in a manner consistent with steady-state testing of a conventional powerplant-only vehicle. The rest results are referred to as steady-state test results here, but the battery state of charge, particularly at 10-mph conditions, may materially influence the test results.

We conducted testing over the 4-bag FTP, HFET, and US06 cycles prior to the steady-state testing referred to below. With the engine warm, the vehicle was driven to 10-mph conditions and this mode was driven for approximately three minutes prior to ten minutes of emission sampling. The vehicle was then driven to 20-mph conditions, a brief stabilization period was allowed, and emissions sampling was conducted for another 10-minute period. This procedure was repeated for 30, 40, and 50 mph conditions. The results from this testing are presented in Table 19, below.

41

Table 19

Toyota Prius Hybrid Vehicle Steady-State Emissions Testing							
Test Mode	FID HC	NMHCE	CO	CO_2	NO_x	FE	Net Charge*
	g/mi	g/mi	g/mi	g/mi	g/mi	MPG	Amp·hrs
10 mph	0.01	0.00	0.1	103	Neg.	83.71	0.205
20 mph	0.03	0.02	0.1	140	0.01	61.66	-0.235
30 mph	0.01	0.01	0.1	134	0.01	64.39	-0.268
40 mph	0.01	0.01	0.2	137	0.00	63.06	0.027
50 mph	0.01	0.00	0.2	156	0.00	55.18	0.241

* Negative values relate to net battery-pack charging over the test cycle; positive values relate to net battery-pack discharge over the cycle.

The THS operated in a battery-only mode for a portion of the 10-mph steady-state test, and a net discharge from the battery was noted. Net charging of the battery occurred during the following 20- and 30-mph modes. CO_2 emissions per mile, and hence, fuel economies, were relatively similar for the 20-, 30-, and 40-mph steady-states, regardless of the amount of battery-pack charging done by the internal combustion engine. Fifty-mph steady-state emission levels approximate those from HFET schedule tests conducted with the THS, and net battery discharging was noted over this 10-minute test. NOx emissions were low during all of this steady-state testing. Fuel economy test results are presented in this section with the caveat that these figures involve conventional vehicle steady-state test procedures, rather than transient cycle operation.

The steady-state mpg values generated can be compared to the mpg values generated during cyclic testing by plotting both values versus average speed. The results presented in Figure 11 show the relationship for the Toyota Prius.

In order of average speed, the cyclic data points included here are average fuel economy figures for the New York City Cycle, Bag 2 of the FTP, the cold start LA-4 (1370 seconds), the SC03 cycle, Bag 1 of the FTP, the US06 cycle, and the HFET cycle. It should be noted that the high fuel economy recorded for the second point (Bag 2 of the FTP) may have been influenced by substantial battery discharge during this segment. Though they are similar in average speed, the HFET and US06 cycles have very different fuel economies associated with them due to the "aggressive" accel/decel nature of the US06 versus the "steadier" HFET cycle.

In general, however, the steady-state fuel economy figures are substantially higher than fuel economies from averages over cyclic driving. This is generally due to the changes in inertia inherent to cyclic driving, deeper charging/discharging of the battery with cyclic driving, and the inability to recover 100 percent of braking energy with the regenerative braking system.

The greatest variance is perhaps indicated at low speed conditions where the start/stop New York Cycle average fuel economy is compared to 10-mph steady-state conditions. (These steady-state conditions are affected by the substantial battery discharge; hence, a lower operational mode for the internal combustion engine.) Between 20 and 40 mph, the steady-state fuel economy is roughly double that obtained as an average over certain transient cycles.

Figure 11
"Steady-State/Cyclic" MPG vs. MPH

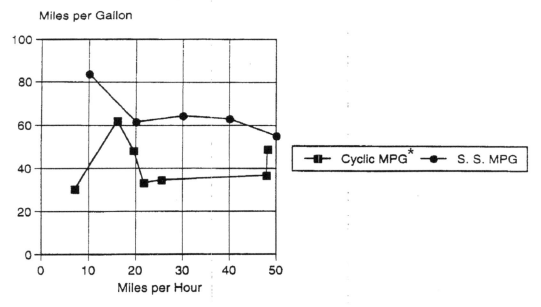

*Cyclic mpg data points here are New York City Cycle, Bag 2 of FTP, cold-start LA-4, SC03 cycle, Bag 1 of FTP, US06 cycle, and HFET cycle, in that order.

I.   Fuel Economy Issues

  1.   Adjustments for Net Charge/Discharge of Battery Pack

  Hybrid electric vehicles must be equipped with an energy
storage system capable of storing energy to drive an electric
motor. This system, a battery pack in the case of the THS, may
be recharged off-vehicle from a power grid, through regenerative
braking energy recovery, or through a recharging circuit onboard
the vehicle. The THS battery pack is normally recharged by a
combination of regenerative braking and the recharging circuit
using the onboard internal combustion engine (see Vehicle
Operating Strategy, above).

  Over a vehicle operating mode such as the 4-Bag FTP, the
battery pack of the charge-sustaining THS may charge and
discharge a number of times, according to the operating strategy.
EPA recorded the net charge/discharge during each testing mode
(see Test Procedures, above). A net charge/discharge of zero
over a test mode may indicate little or no change in the state of
charge of the battery pack. (This may depend upon the state of
charge when the charging/discharging occurred, however.) A net
discharge of the battery over a test mode may indicate less
demand placed on the internal combustion engine powerplant during
that mode compared to a "zero" charge/discharge. If fuel economy
is calculated in a "conventional" manner for a charge-sustaining
hybrid such as the THS, (using emissions data from the internal
combustion engine), a net battery discharge will overstate fuel
economy. Conversely, a net battery charge during a test cycle
may understate conventionally calculated fuel economy.

  Toyota suggested a factor to adjust fuel economy for a net
charge/discharge over a test cycle.[3] This method involves the
generation of a multiplier, described by Toyota as a "k" factor,
to apply against unadjusted fuel economy. The "k" factor would
relate fuel economy to charging/discharging over a test cycle,
and its application would seek to adjust fuel economy to a "zero"
net charge/discharge level. EPA plotted net charge/discharge
over several test modes against unadjusted fuel economy to
determine relationships between battery charging and fuel economy
for the THS.

  Figure 12 relates fuel economy to net charge/discharge for
several tests conducted over the 4-Bag FTP. A straight line
curve fit using regression analysis was used to generate the
trend line described here.

Figure 12
4-Bag FTP Fuel Economy vs. Net Battery Charge/Discharge

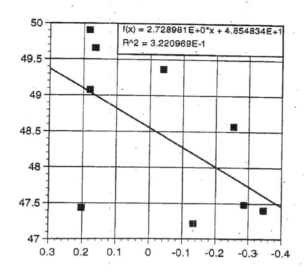

For the range of charge/discharge here, the fuel economy data exhibit a high degree of scatter. A y-intercept of about 48.55 mpg for zero net charge over the 4-Bag FTP is described. A simple average of the fuel economy data points plotted (from Table 6) is 48.45 mpg. Therefore, if a zero net battery charge/discharge fuel economy description was required, on the basis of the data presented here, the answer might be close to a simple average of the data.

This data might be used to generate a factor to adjust the fuel economies of individual tests which have non-zero net battery-pack charge/discharge recorded. Table 20 adjusts the fuel economies of the "unadjusted" data in Figure 12. The adjustment factor is the slope of the line in Figure 12, or 2.729 mpg (net amp·hours). Fuel economies with net battery charging noted over the cycle are adjusted upward, while those with net discharges are adjusted downward.

Table 20

Toyota Prius THS			
Fuel Economies Adjusted for Net Battery Charge/Discharge 4-Bag FTP Cycle			
Test Date	4-Bag FTP Cycle	Net Charge/ Discharge*	"Adjusted" Fuel Economy
	MPG	Amp·hrs	MPG
3/27/98	49.07	0.191	48.54
3/28/98	47.43	0.203	46.88
3/31/98	47.40	-0.344	48.34
4/1/98	49.65	0.166	49.20
4/2/98	49.94	0.184	49.44
4/3/98	47.48	-0.285	48.26
4/17/98	48.57	-0.252	49.26
4/23/98	47.21	-0.132	47.57
4/24/98	49.36	-0.038	49.47

* Negative values relate to net battery-pack charging over the test cycle; positive values relate to net battery-pack discharge over the cycle.

The magnitude of the adjustments that would be made by this method range from 0.55 mpg (subtractive) to 0.94 mpg (additive). The largest adjustment amounts to a slightly greater than two-percent boost in fuel economy.

Tests conducted over the HFET cycle following a 4-Bag FTP (Test Sequence No. 2) were characterized by substantial battery-pack recharging during the cycle. No HFET immediately following an FTP test exhibited net battery-pack discharging.

HFET fuel economy for the HFET conducted immediately following a 4-Bag FTP are graphed below in Figure 13, versus net battery pack charging in amp·hours. The trend line here is constructed in the same manner as described earlier for Figure 12.

Figure 13
HFET Fuel Economy vs. Net Battery Charge/Discharge
(Test Sequence No. 2)

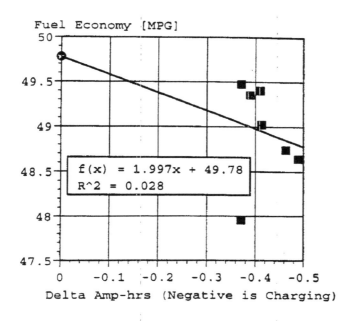

○ = MPG Zero Net-Charging

   A great deal of scatter in this data is apparent, though the
range of net battery charging is only 0.370 amp·hours through
0.489 amp·hours. The extrapolated zero net charge/discharge fuel
economy value is 49.78 mpg. An adjustment of each individual
test in the manner described above would have the effect of
raising the reported fuel economy for each data point given here,
as each point involved net battery-pack charging. Table 21,
below, lists the adjustments to the individual HFET cycle tests
(Test Sequence No. 2 procedure) suggested by this method.

Table 21

Toyota Prius THS			
HFET Tests, Sequence No. 2 Test Procedure Fuel Economy Adjusted for Net Battery Charge			
Test Date	HFET	Net Battery Charge*	"Adjusted" Fuel Economy
	MPG	Amp·hrs	MPG
3/25/98	48.75	-0.462	49.67
3/31/98	49.48	-0.370	50.22
4/1/98	49.41	-0.409	50.22
4/2/98	49.03	-0.412	49.85
4/3/98	48.65	-0.488	49.62
4/23/98	47.96	-0.370	48.70
4/24/98	49.36	-0.388	50.13

* Negative values relate to net battery-pack charging over the test cycle;
positive values relate to net battery-pack discharge over the cycle.

Figure 14, below, presents HFET mpg for the second HFET
following a 4-Bag FTP test (Test Sequence No. 1, see Test
Procedures, above) versus net battery pack charging/ discharging.

Figure 14
HFET Fuel Economy vs. Net Battery Charge/Discharge
(Test Sequence No. 1)

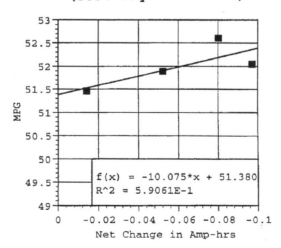

This data appears to show an unexpected relationship between battery-pack charging and fuel economy, i.e., lower fuel economy with lower battery charging. No reason is given here for this unexpected relationship, other than general test variability. An adjustment factor based on this relationship would have the effect of lowering reported fuel economy values for tests with net battery charging exhibited. Further testing would have to be conducted to explain this relationship.

Toyota suggested that EPA should combine the data in Figures 13 and 14 (HFET data) in order to determine a fuel economy adjustment factor or net zero charging fuel economy value for HFET testing. This was suggested because of the clustering of data around two net charging values for the HFET in these figures. Figure 13 refers to the first HFET following the 4-Bag FTP (Test Sequence No. 2) while Figure 14 refers to the second HFET after the 4-Bag FTP (Test Sequence No. 1). These tests, both using the HFET cycle, are nevertheless dissimilar because of the difference in time sequence when they are conducted. EPA believes it may be misleading to include both sets of data in a graph to determine an adjustment factor because of this time difference.

2. "Running" Fuel Economy

Another way to express fuel economy is actual miles driven versus actual gallons consumed. This method is illustrated in Table 22, where miles driven and gallons of fuel consumed over the 4-Bag FTP and EPA-suggested HFET, immediately following the FTP, are presented. Fuel economy calculated in this manner has the effect of eliminating the conventional cold/hot weighting factors. A "composite" fuel economy based on dividing total miles driven versus gallons of fuel consumed is given for each test. A running average of fuel economy calculated in this manner for these tests is also given. The "running average" fuel economy calculated in this manner slightly exceeds 48 mpg.

Table 22

Toyota Prius THS "Running" Fuel Economy - Actual Miles/Actual Gallons Test Sequence No. 2 FTP/HFET Cycle						
Test Date	Miles	Gallons	Test Average MPG	Cumulative Miles	Cumulative Gallons	Cumulative MPG
03/25/98	25.189	0.5241	48.06	25.189	0.5241	48.06
03/27/98	25.161	0.5124	49.10	50.350	1.0365	48.58
03/28/98	25.028	0.5254	47.64	75.378	1.5619	48.26
03/31/98	25.041	0.5228	47.90	100.419	2.0847	48.17
04/01/98	25.012	0.5072	49.31	125.431	2.5919	48.39
04/02/98	25.041	0.5061	49.47	150.472	3.0980	48.57
04/03/98	25.041	0.5255	47.65	175.513	3.6235	48.06
04/23/98	25.055	0.5310	47.18	200.568	4.1545	48.58
04/24/98	25.109	0.5156	48.70	225.677	4.6701	48.26

Table 23 depicts "conventionally" calculated mpg for Test Sequence No. 2 versus "composite" fuel economy using the conventional city/highway weighting of actual miles driven/fuel consumed for the city/highway tests. The conventionally calculated composite city/highway fuel economies only slightly exceed the composite values calculated using actual miles/gallons for the city and highway values.

This calculation also eliminates the traditional cold/hot city test weighting factors but calculates composite mpg with the traditional 45/55 weighting factors.

Table 23

Table 23

Test Date	"Conventionally "Calculated Composite MPG	Total MPG City *	Total MPG Highway *	Composite Miles/Gallons MPG
Toyota Prius THS — Composite City/Highway Fuel Economy — Conventionally Calculated vs. Actual Miles/Gallons				
03/25/98	48.47	47.59	48.75	47.80
03/27/98	49.36	48.68	49.71	48.64
03/28/98	48.02	46.89	48.75	47.49
03/31/98	48.31	46.86	49.48	47.44
04/01/98	49.54	49.25	49.48	48.86
04/02/98	49.53	49.80	49.41	49.24
04/03/98	48.00	47.00	48.65	47.63
04/23/98	47.54	46.67	47.96	47.38
04/24/98	49.02	48.74	48.62	48.55

* Actual miles vs. actual gallons

Table 24

Overall Fuel Economy Summary			
Test Procedure	Adjusted for State of Charge	MPG	From
Test Sequence No. 2	No Yes	48.6 49.1	Table 8 Figures 12/13
Test Sequence No. 1	No	49.8	Table 11
Miles/Gallons	No	48.3	Table 22

Table 24 presents a summary of some of the many ways that fuel economy was analyzed in this report, showing that for several approaches, the overall mpg for the Prius is between 48 and 50 mpg.

3. Comparison of the Fuel Economy and Emissions of the Prius to Other Vehicles

Since there are other vehicles that get about the same fuel economy that the Prius does, it is of interest to compare the emissions of those other high fuel economy production vehicles to that measured from the Prius. All emissions data used for the comparison are low mileage data.

Table 25

High Fuel Economy Vehicles Comparison of Emission							
Vehicle	Car Class	Test Wt	HC	CO	NO_x	Composite MPG	Transmission
Suzuki Metro	Sub-compact	2125	0.04	0.3	0.04	54.5	M5
VW New Beetle	Sub-compact	3125	0.02	0.1	0.69	51.6	M5
VW Passat	Mid-size	3375	0.22	0.5	0.62	50.4	M5
VW Jetta	Compact	3125	0.10	0.4	0.59	50.9	M5
Toyota Prius	Sub-compact	3000	0.06	0.5	0.05	48.6	AT (THS)
Toyota Corolla	Compact	2750	0.18	1.2	0.12	36.5	M5

The low mileage emissions for the high fuel economy cars are not so far from each other except for NOx. The higher NOx values in the table are all associated with the VW vehicles, all of which are Diesels, and they are more than an order of magnitude higher in NOx than the Prius.

The fuel economy of the Prius can also be compared to a vehicle of the same weight class and the same volume-based size class. Figures 15 and 16 show how the Prius compares to model year 1998 vehicles in the 3000-lb weight class and the subcompact car class, respectively.

The Prius is 64-percent better in fuel economy than the average 3000-lb car, and 66-percent better in fuel economy than the average subcompact car.

The roughly 65-percent improvement in fuel economy shown by the Toyota Prius, compared to the average of other vehicles, is a comparison in which either weight class or car class was held constant. It is very likely that the Toyota Prius has slower 0-60 mph acceleration performance than the average vehicles in the two classes, since the average 0-60 time for vehicles in the 3000-lb weight class is estimated to be 10.5 seconds and for the subcompact car class, 10.2 seconds. The 0-60 time measured for the Prius on the chassis dynamometer is 14.2 seconds using the average of the six tests with the 20-second braking protocol.

If one accounts for the performance difference between the Toyota Prius and the average 3000-lb car and the average subcompact car, the fuel economy advantage of the Toyota Prius is reduced to a 45-percent increase.

4.   What About the 66-mpg Value Associated With This Car?

When the Prius vehicle was introduced as a commercial product in Japan, the fuel economy when tested over the Japanese test procedure also became available. Indeed, the brochure on the Prius, provided to EPA as part of the background information on the vehicle, quoted fuel efficiency <u>on the Japanese 10-15 city driving mode</u> of 28.0 km/liter. Converting to mpg:

$$\frac{28.0 km}{\ell} \ x \ \frac{mile}{1.609 km} \ x \ \frac{3.785 liters}{gallon} = 65.9 MPG$$

or
about 66 mpg. This 66-mpg value is even cited in Toyota's press release of December 11, 1997--without the caveat that the results were obtained on a test cycle substantially different from the one used in the U.S. to measure and report fuel economy. Others, for example *Business Week*, December 15, 1997, page 108, picked up this and other information and also reported the 66-mpg value.

Figure 15
Distribution of MY98 55/45 MPG
3000 Pound Inertia Weight Class

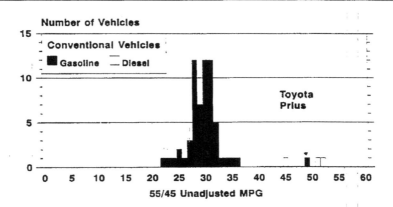

Figure 16
Distribution of MY98 55/45 MPG
EPA Subcompact Class

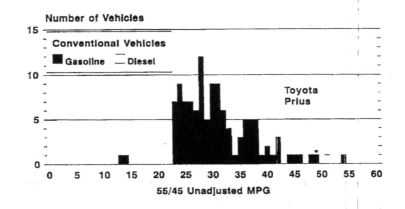

The necessary clarification needed is to remember that fuel economy results always need to be referenced to the specific test method by which they were derived. This has not been an issue in the U.S. for more than 25 years, since the Federal Trade Commission ruled that only EPA fuel economy values could be used for advertising. So when people in the U.S. now see fuel-economy values cited, it is logical to assume that they think it is a U.S. test-based value. The 66 mpg for the Prius is not. It is a value determined on the Japanese 10-15 mode procedure which has historically yielded higher fuel economy values than the official U.S. test.

The fuel economy results reported in this report are consistent with the driving cycles and calculation procedures used to determine fuel economy in the U.S.

EPA tested the Prius vehicle on California Phase-II gasoline, at Toyota's request. Current Federal vehicle certification uses a correction factor that takes into account fuel properties to adjust calculated volumetric fuel economy when Phase-II fuel is used. The fuel economies presented in this report are unadjusted. To express these fuel economies in the adjusted manner currently used in the certification process, each fuel economy value would have to be increased by about one percent.

The most current properties of the test fuel indicate a net heat of combustion, by ASTM D3338, of 18518 BTU/lb. The specific gravity of the fuel, 0.7402, indicates a value of 114,430 BTU/gallon, approximately 0.26 percent higher than the baseline fuel. On the basis of the BTU content of the fuel alone, this would mean that the fuel economies presented in this report would have to be adjusted downward, multiplying the reported figures by a factor of 0.9974.

55

VII. Highlights from Testing

1.   The THS was evaluated over two test sequences involving the Federal Urban Dynamometer Driving Schedule and the Highway Fuel Economy Test.   These tests are described in Figure 6 and 7, Test Procedures, and the Discussion of Test Results, above.

Test Sequence No. 1 involved a 4-Bag FTP followed immediately by a conditioning HFET and a second, measured HFET. Measured emissions of hydrocarbons, carbon monoxide, and oxides of nitrogen were well below the current Federal standards for gasoline-fueled light-duty vehicles.   The average composite city/highway fuel economy measured over Test Sequence No. 2 was 48.6.   The average composite city/highway fuel economy measured over Test Sequence No. 1 was 49.8.   Both of these figures are uncorrected for state of charge or battery-pack charging/discharging over the test cycles.

2.   Limited performance testing (0-60 mph acceleration testing) was conducted. With a normally charged battery pack, an average 0-60 mph time of slightly over 14 seconds was noted. This time increased to about 19.5 seconds with the battery pack discharged well below what Toyota considers a normal state of charge.

3.   A number of tests over the HFET cycle in succession were conducted.   The average fuel economy over the HFET, following "conditioning drives" over several HFET cycles, was about ⁼3.8 mpg.   This fuel economy figure ignores state of battery charge or charging/discharging of the battery over the tests.

4.   Several tests in succession over the US06 driving cycle were conducted.   Some of these tests were conducted with the battery pack in a state of deeper than normal discharge prior to commencement of testing. A relationship between the state of charge of the battery pack and the ability of the THS to follow precisely the aggressive driving trace of the US06 was noted.

5.   An attempt to relate net battery charging/discharging over a test cycle or driving mode was made by EPA. Battery state of charge, or in the absence of that measurement, net battery charge/discharge over a driving cycle is important if fuel economy and emissions are calculated in a conventional manner,

examining emissions from the engine only from a charge-sustaining hybrid electric vehicle. Measured fuel economy over Test Sequence No. 2 versus net battery charging/discharging over these modes was presented in Figures 12 and 13. A relationship between these two parameters using linear least squares regression was established. The predicted value of 4-Bag FTP or "city" fuel economy relating to a zero net charge/discharge over this test cycle was 48.5 mpg. The predicted fuel economy for the HFET (Test Sequence No. 2) immediately following a 4-Bag FTP relating to a zero net charge/discharge of the battery pack was 49.8 mpg.

VIII. Acknowledgments

The authors gratefully acknowledge the Toyota Motor Corporation and the Toyota Technical Center, U.S.A., for providing the THS and technical support for this evaluation.

The authors acknowledge the efforts of Robert Moss, Testing Services Division (TSD), EPA, who drove the vehicle over all testing referred to here. Carl Paulina, TSD, served as test coordinator for TSD, and William Courtois, TSD, processed the test results and programmed the necessary special driver's traces.

The following individuals served as emissions analyzer operators during the THS evaluation: Darlene Curtis, Philip Conde, Scott Wilson, Jeff Cieslak, all of TSD. Special recognition is also given to Peter Forgacs, TSD, for outstanding and timely electronics support.

The authors also acknowledge Robert Heavenrich, David Swain, Lillian Johnson, and Robert Kelly of the Advanced Technology Support Division (ATSD), EPA, who provided comparison fuel economy data, provided battery characteristics, typed this manuscript, and provided electronics support, respectively.

IX. References

1. Toyota Electric and Hybrid Vehicles, Toyota Motor Corporation International Communications Dept., Tokyo, Japan, December 1997.

2. "Toyota Hybrid System," 1997 Press Information, Toyota Motor Corporation, International Public Affairs Division, Toyota City, Japan, May 1997.

3. Letter, Matsubara, A., Toyota Motor Corporation, to Oge, M., U.S. EPA, February 3, 1998.

4. "Recommended Practice For Measuring The Exhaust Emissions and Fuel Economy of Hybrid-Electric Vehicles," Society of Automotive Engineers (SAE) Procedure J1711 (Draft), February 4, 1998.

5. "Proposed California Air Resources Board Hybrid Electric Vehicle Test Procedures," Draft, California Air Resources Board, El Monte, CA, April 3, 1998.

6. "Exhaust Emission Test Procedure for SC03 Emissions," 40 CFR, Part 86, Section 160-00, dtd July 1, 1997.

Appendix A

Test Vehicle Specifications
Toyota Hybrid System (THS)

Vehicle Type	Toyota Prius 4-Door Sedan
Seating Capacity	5
Interior Volume	98.6 ft^3
Vehicle Class	Subcompact
Vehicle Length	4.275 m
Vehicle Height	1.490 m
Vehicle Width	1.695 m
Wheelbase	2.550 m
Tire Pressure	32 psi
Curb Weight	2783 lbs (w/full fuel tank)
Vehicle Inertia	
Test Weight	3000 lbs
Dynamometer	
Set Coefficients	A = 7.12 lbs
(Parasitic Drag	B = -0.0971 lbs/mph
or Windage)	C = 0.02078 lbs/mph^2

Appendix B

THS Internal Combustion Engine Specifications

Cylinders	4
Displacement	1.5 liters
Bore	75 mm
Stroke	84.7 mm
Mechanical Compression Ratio	9.0:1
Expansion Ratio	13.5:1
Valve Train	4-Valve, Dual Overhead Cam incorporates Toyota Variable Valve Timing with Intelligence (VVT-i)
Combustion Chamber	Pentroof Design
Ignition	Toyota Direct Ignition
Fuel System	Electronic Sequential Port Fuel Injection
Maximum Engine Speed	4000 rpm
Power	Maximum 43 kW at 4000 rpm

Features: The engine uses all-aluminum head and block construction. The engine incorporates modified Atkinson cycle operation, with late intake-valve closure, to enable a lower effective compression ratio, when compared to the expansion ratio. Toyota claims a "thinner" crankshaft, lower tensile strength piston rings, and reduced valve spring loads for this engine compared to a "comparable" 1.5-liter, 4-valve engine. These economies are enabled as a result of the reduced engine speed (maximum 4000 rpm) and output of this engine compared to similar engines, it is claimed by Toyota. Detailed specifications are available from the Toyota Motor Corporation.

19-Mar-98   NVFEL Fuel Analysis Report   CA Phase II 2/23/98   Page 1 of 2

CA Phase II 2/23/98

Facility Name: UE EPA NVFEL Fuels Group   Facility Type: In house

Owner: US EPA   Phone: (734) 741-7881

2565 Plymouth Road

Ann Arbor, MI 48105   Washtenaw County

Inspector: NST   Inspection Date : 2/23/98   Time In: 00:00 Time Out: 00:00

Samples Type: Test Fuel

Inspection information logged in by PAB on 2/23/98.

CA Phase II 2/23/98 FTAG: 6960   Comments: Leaked: No

Test Code	Test Method		Results	Units	Possible Violation ?	Analyst	Analysis Date
62	Vapor Pressure by Appendix E Method 3		6.92	PSIA	No	PAB	2/23/98
62	Vapor Pressure by Appendix E Method 3		6.92	PSIA	No	PAB	2/23/98
692	Degrees API		59.64	Degrees API	No	PAB	2/23/98
691	Specific Gravity @ 60 Degrees F		0.73954	g/mL @ 60 F	No	PAB	2/23/98
69	Density @ 60 deg F		0.74027	g/cm-03 @ 60 deg F	No	PAB	2/23/98
101	D 86	Initial Boiling Point	98.3	Degrees F	No	PAB	2/23/98
101	D 86	Initial Boiling Point	97.59	Degrees F	No	PAB	2/23/98
101	D 86	Initial Boiling Point	99.69	Degrees F	No	PAB	2/23/98
110		10 Percent	141.39	Degrees F	No	PAB	2/23/98
110		10 Percent	141.69	Degrees F	No	PAB	2/23/98
110		10 Percent	139.3	Degrees F	No	PAB	2/23/98
150		50 Percent	208.8	Degrees F	No	PAB	2/23/98
150		50 Percent	207.5	Degrees F	No	PAB	2/23/98
150		50 Percent	209.5	Degrees F	No	PAB	2/23/98
190		90 Percent	300.29	Degrees F	No	PAB	2/23/98
190		90 Percent	300.1	Degrees F	No	PAB	2/23/98
190		90 Percent	298.39	Degrees F	No	PAB	2/23/98
200		End Point	377.7	Degrees F	No	PAB	2/23/98
200		End Point	391.79	Degrees F	No	PAB	2/23/98
200		End Point	390.39	Degrees F	No	PAB	2/23/98
201		Residue	1	mL	No	PAB	2/23/98
201		Residue	0.8	mL	No	PAB	2/23/98
201		Residue	1.29	mL	No	PAB	2/23/98
202		Total Recovery	98.59	mL	No	PAB	2/23/98
202		Total Recovery	98.3	mL	No	PAB	2/23/98
202		Total Recovery	97.5	mL	No	PAB	2/23/98
203		Loss	0.6	mL	No	PAB	2/23/98
203		Loss	1.2	mL	No	PAB	2/23/98
203		Loss	0.69	mL	No	PAB	2/23/98
65		Percent Evaporated at 200 Degrees F	46	Volume Percent	No	PAB	2/23/98
65		Percent Evaporated at 200 Degrees F	45	Volume Percent	No	PAB	2/23/98

NVFEL Fuel Analysis Report

Percent Evaporated at 200 Degrees F	45.29 Volume Percent	No	PAB	2/23/98
Percent Evaporated at 300 Degrees F	89.9 Volume Percent	No	PAB	2/23/98
Percent Evaporated at 300 Degrees F	90 Volume Percent	No	PAB	2/23/98
Percent Evaporated at 300 Degrees F	90.19 Volume Percent	No	PAB	2/23/98
Olefins in Petro. Prod. by ASTM D 1319-93	6.77 Volume Percent	No	NST	3/16/98
Aromatics in Petro. Prod. by ASTM 1319-93	23.7 Volume Percent	No	NST	3/16/98
Methanol by MSD (Screen)	0 Volume Percent	No	EL	2/25/98
Methanol by MSD (Screen)	0 Volume Percent	No	EL	2/25/98
MTBE by MSD (Screen)	11.6 Volume Percent	No	EL	2/25/98
MTBE by MSD (Screen)	11.8 Volume Percent	No	EL	2/25/98
ETBE by MSD (Screen)	0 Volume Percent	No	EL	2/25/98
ETBE by MSD (Screen)	0 Volume Percent	No	EL	2/25/98
TAME by MSD (Screen)	0 Volume Percent	No	EL	2/25/98
TAME by MSD (Screen)	0 Volume Percent	No	EL	2/25/98
Volume Percent Oxygenates by MSD (Screen)	11.8 Volume Percent	No	EL	2/25/98
Volume Percent Oxygenates by MSD (Screen)	11.6 Volume Percent	No	EL	2/25/98
Weight Percent Oxygen by MSD (Screen)	2.11 Weight Percent	No	EL	2/25/98
Weight Percent Oxygen by MSD (Screen)	2.16 Weight Percent	No	EL	2/25/98
Benzene in Gasoline by MSD D5769	0.727 Volume Percent	No	EL	2/25/98
Benzene in Gasoline by MSD D5769	0.73 Volume Percent	No	EL	2/25/98
Aromatics in Gasoline by MSD D5769	24.26 Volume Percent	No	EL	2/25/98
Aromatics in Gasoline by MSD D5769	24.75 Volume Percent	No	EL	2/25/98
Benzene in Gasoline by ASTM D 3606	0.7179 Volume Percent	No	TW	2/27/98
Methanol by OFID	0 Volume Percent	No	YTS	2/25/98
Methanol by OFID	0 Volume Percent	No	YTS	2/25/98
Ethanol by OFID	0 Volume Percent	No	YTS/TW	2/25/98
Ethanol by OFID	0 Volume Percent	No	YTS/TW	2/25/98
Ethanol by MSD (Screen)	0 Volume Percent	No	EL	2/25/98
Ethanol by MSD (Screen)	0 Volume Percent	No	EL	2/25/98
t-Butanol by OFID	0 Volume Percent	No	YTS/TW	2/25/98
t-Butanol by OFID	0 Volume Percent	No	YTS/TW	2/25/98
TAME by OFID	0.2 Volume Percent	No	YTS/TW	2/25/98
TAME by OFID	0.16 Volume Percent	No	YTS/TW	2/25/98
Volume Percent Oxygenates by OFID	10.91 Volume Percent	No	YTS/TW	2/25/98
Volume Percent Oxygenates by OFID	11.06 Volume Percent	No	YTS/TW	2/25/98
Weight Percent Oxygen by OFID	2.02 Weight Percent	No	YTS/TW	2/25/98
Weight Percent Oxygen by OFID	1.99 Weight Percent	No	YTS/TW	2/25/98
Sulfur in Gasoline by ASTM D 2622	13 Parts Per Million	No	AJA	2/23/98

Lightning Source UK Ltd.
Milton Keynes UK
UKHW050718171218
334136UK00005B/265/P